"WHISTLING POPS"

*T*his book title, "Whistling Pops" came to me while thinking about the years gone by.

I pictured an old man going for a walk, with his hands behind his back, whistling a tune. Sometimes his head may be up, looking at the sky, maybe an attempt to feel proud and satisfied, as he thinks about his many accomplishments, with his family and friends and his devotion to his job and how grateful he is to have walked this earth. Sometimes his head is down as he walks, perhaps feeling a bit curious, regretful or wondering of the roads ahead.

So to this very elegant man going for his walk, sometimes lucky enough to be walking with his wife of many years, holding hands, as they both whisper to each other, exchanging love memories about when their lives first began with each other, maybe one day while the soft wind blows in the warmth of a summer sky, we too will be going for that walk of life, wondering how it all went by so fast and did we do our best.

When that moment of true self kicks in and the perpetual light is about to show us the way to our final rest, remember him. Remember Pops and how he whistled.

AuthorHouse™ LLC
1663 Liberty Drive
Bloomington, IN 47403
www.authorhouse.com
Phone: 1-800-839-8640

Published by AuthorHouse   09/29/2014

ISBN: 978-1-4969-4347-7 (sc)
ISBN: 978-1-4969-4346-0 (e)

Library of Congress Control Number: 2014917430

*A*lso Author of, "*On Faith We Fly*" and "*The Bells Of Humility*", both books published by AuthorHouse Publishing, Bloomington, Indiana, U.S.A.

authorHOUSE®

Dedicated to the DeCarteret College 1973
Adidas Cup, All-Island Private School Champions,
Jamaica National Stadium, Kingston, Jamaica.

An Honour never forgotten.

CONTENTS

PREFACE

Many things in life can give us the inspiration to write. One great inspiration of mine resulted in the value of a smile. In 1991, the Royal Yacht Britannia came to Toronto for a visit from the Royal Family. I was doing a Security detail for this event and was lucky enough to be directing traffic, when Princess Diana was being driven to an event. The vehicle that she was in made a sharp turn from a driveway onto the main roadway. The vehicle passed me by just a few feet away and there in the back seat, sat a Princess. Princess Diana. I looked right at her and smiled and waved to her. She looked back at me and smiled and waved. She was everything in beauty that one could ever imagine. So elegant, so kind, so charming. I have never forgotten that smile and that wave and the effect that it had on me.

Another inspiration of mine has been meeting my biological mother. We met for the first time at a Mall in Montreal. While I stood and waited for her inside a busy weekend Mall, from quite a distance away, I could see this very beautiful lady with a big smile, my smile, with a sparkle in her eyes that could light up the Universe. I needed that smile from my mother, to take me through those times when you just needed to make it all better. It was to last me the rest of my life.

As I write, I have tried to use positive words, situations, dreams, events, so as to try and let them be an inspiration to others, as I know the positive effect that it can have on people. If one day, someone can pick up one of my books and smile, or cry a tear of joy or remembrance, than I have been privileged to have been a part of your day, that has made you feel good about this world that we have been so blessed to be in.

So if I had to do it all again, given the same circumstances, I would do it the same. I would take great value from my inspirations and use them to build my fortress of life. Many years ago, a close family member once repeated the phrase that I had never heard before; "When you are a child, the whole world is yours". Such a powerful statement that I needed to hear at that time. I asked her to write it on a piece of paper for me and I kept that in my wallet for many years.

So I write for you, the people, the ones I Love.

A KIND SEASON

WHEN I FOUND THE FREEDOM TO BE ME
THE HAZE LIFTED,
WHEN I FOUND THE VALUE IN DIFFERENCE
THE WORDS THAWED,
WHEN THE WINDS OF TIME SLOWED MY WILL
I TOOK SHELTER IN THE FOG,
WHEN I BEGAN TO UNDERSTAND EQUALITY
I BEGAN TO APPRECIATE THE FOUR SEASONS,
WHEN I BEGAN TO CRY
I WATCHED THE RAINS GIVE LIFE,
WHEN I WAS LOST
THE TREES WERE MY SHELTER,
WHEN I NEEDED MY THOUGHTS
THE STILL WINDS GAVE ME PEACE,
WHEN I LOVED
THE SUN WARMED MY HEART,
WHILE I SLEPT THROUGH DARK TIMES
YOU WERE MY BRIGHTEST DREAM.

A PIER TO SEA

I OFTEN THOUGHT OF THAT PIER,
WHEN I SAW ALL SEA LIFE IN ONE WATER,
IN ONE BIG SCHOOL
MERMAIDS LIKE A PRINCESS DAUGHTER,
REFLECTIONS ON THE WATER TOP
SCENTED WEEDS AND DRIFTWOOD DROP,
IMAGINATIONS BAND, ALL SEASIDE SAND,
I WANTED MORE, TO SWIM WITH FISH
A DOLPHIN WAS MY BIRTHDAY WISH,
I FELT THE PEACEFUL OCEAN SPRAYS
THE OVERCAST AND SUNNY DAYS,
ALONG THE PIER, I HAD NO FEAR
I HEARD THE SEAGULLS SPEAK,
I SAW THE FLIGHT FROM BUOY TO BOAT
WITH FISH STILL IN HIS BEAK,
THE WATER ROLLS AND FISHING POLES
THE WAVES THAT SWIM TO SHORE,
THE JELLY FISH AND OYSTER DISH
I ALWAYS WANTED MORE,
SO AS I SAIL THE SEAS OF LIFE
THE COLOURED WINDS OF ART,
IM DRAWN TOWARDS THAT PRECIOUS PIER
THAT'S WRITTEN ON MY HEART.

A TIME I KNEW

As I SAT AND WATCHED THE MORNING SUN
AND HEARD THE NIGHTLY NEWS,
THE YEARS HAD PASSED, MORE QUESTIONS ASKED
THE SLOWER YEARS I CHOOSE,
MY WORKING DAYS NOW JUST A HAZE
AS I MOVE TOWARD NEW TIME,
MY PIPE IN HAND, I STARE THE LAND
THE QUIET HAS BEEN KIND,
NOT MANY FRIENDS AS EACH DAY ENDS
I GUESS THEIR DRIFTING TOO,
AS WE PREPARE FOR NEXT IN LINE
TO SEE LIFES JOURNEY THROUGH,
THE SOULS THAT TOIL, THE SEEDS IN SOIL
THEY STRUGGLE FOR THE CAUSE,
PREPARE FOR FUTURE HAPPY TIMES
COULD PASS IN JUST A PAUSE,
MY ROCKING CHAIR HAS NO COMPARE
IT WINDS MY WONDER SKIES,
THE QUESTIONS OF OUR FUTURE AGE
EACH MORNING, WILL WE RISE,
IVE DONE MY BEST TO LAY MY BED
AND RAISED MY HEAD, NO STRIFE,
NOW I CAN SEE, MY LEGACY
MY SONS, MY DAUGHTER AND MY WIFE.

BANDITS COLOURED BELLS OF GREEN

I DARED TO WALK THE PLANKS OF FATE
TO VIEW THE GODS OF PRECIOUS GOWNS,
LUCKY NUMBERS, FRUITS OF FIELDS
MANY LIKES AND ROWS OF CLOWNS,
DIFFERENT WAYS AT DIFFERENT TIMES
MORE MUSIC THAN THE NURSERY RHYMES,
THE LIGHTS THAT DAZZLE AND SURPRISE
THE WINNING SUNSETS CAST THOSE DREAMS,
WITH EVERY NOTE MY HOPES TO RISE
THE FEW THAT FALL, THERES MORE IT SEEMS,
ANOTHER CHORUS SINGS ITS WINNING WAYS
THE TIDES COME IN, THE MOON IS BRIGHT
THE ROLLING GOLDENS DRAW MORE PRAISE
THIS DAY IS MINE AND SO IS NIGHT,
ALL WAITING FOR THE WINNING SONG
SPECIAL COLOURS WITH EVERY QUEST,
WHEN TIMES SEEM RIGHT THERE COULD BE WRONG
THIS IS MY TIME, THIS IS MY NEST,
THOUGH SWEETEST STORIES EVER TOLD
THE LUCKY FEW ARE SELDOM SEEN,
THE FEW THAT PLAY THE DEVILS GAMES
WILL TEST THE COLOURED BELLS OF GREEN.

BRIDGES OF OUR BRAVE

THE MOVING HIGHWAY PASSES BY
I HEAR THE FIELDS WHERE HEROES LAY,
MY EYES TOWARD THE SKY IN PRAYER
GOD BLESS THIS SOUL UPON THIS DAY,
AS SILENCE WATCHES OVER US
WE LOOK OUT TOWARD THE BRAVE,
THE FLASHING RED ESCORT OUR OWN
THE HONOUR OF OUR FLAGS THAT WAVE,
FROM EVERY WALK WE STAND WITH PRIDE
TO SEE OUR LOVED ONES FINAL RIDE,
AND AS THEY PASS, OUR HANDS TO HEART
A COUNTRY JOINED BY ALL THE STARS,
THE UNIFORM THAT'S LAID TO REST
GOD BLESS THIS CHILD, FOR THIS ONES OURS.

CARDINAL RULE

*I*T'S TIME TO FLY MY LITTLE ONE
FOR YOU TO TEST YOU'RE WINGS,
IT'S TIME FOR YOU TO SEE THE WORLD
WHATEVER YOUR LIFE BRINGS,
THOUGH YOU MAY FALL, YOU'RE WINGS AND ALL
AGAINST A LONELY SKY,
TO SEE THE LEAVES OF FALLEN TREES
DETERMINES HOW YOU FLY,
THE NEST IS BARE FOR ALL ARE GONE
NOW YOU MUST FLOAT WITH MIGHT,
THE TINY TWIGS AND BITS OF STRAW
WILL KEEP YOU WARM AT NIGHT,
TAKE TO A BRANCH THAT'S REALLY HIGH
SO YOU CAN SEE THE PREY,
YOU'RE EYES AROUND, WITHOUT A SOUND
TO FLY ANOTHER DAY,
SO SPREAD YOUR WINGS MY LITTLE BIRD
BEFORE THE WINTER COMES,
AND LEARN THE WINDS OF OPEN SKIES
TO BUILD YOU'RE NEST WITH LITTLE ONES.

DIME WILL TELL

*T*HE SHANTY DIME UPON THE GROUND
AS THOUGH YOU SLEEP A WINK,
I SEE YOU LOST FOR WORDS AND PATH
SHOULD I PICK UP, I THINK,

WHERE WAS YOUR LAST OF HOMES I SAY
AND WERE YOU THROWN OR DROPPED,
POOR SOUL WITHOUT THAT FAITHFUL DIME
THERE BUDGET NOW BEEN CHOPPED,

BEEN STEPPED UPON AND KICKED A BIT
IT'S MOVED ACROSS THE LOT,
SMALL CHANGE TO SOME, NOT EVERYONE
THERES THOSE, ITS ALL THEY GOT,

SO NOW YOU'RE MINE YOU FALLEN FRIEND
OR THROWN AWAY IT SEEMS,
MY PRIDE AND YOU FULFIL MY QUEST
TO HELP ME REACH MY DREAMS.

FAIRWAYS OF MY FATHER

THROUGH CHILL AND SWEAT I WALKED THE MILES
I BRAVED EACH COURSE I PLAYED,
THE STROKES OF LIFE THAT TURNED TO ME
I TOILED AND PAR WAS MADE,
THE WATERFALLS WITH NATURES CALLS
THAT CALMED MY INNER ME,
WITH EVERY STRIDE, OR SHOOTING WIDE
I LOVED MY FAMILY,
SOME GREENS WERE MADE AND SOME WERE NOT
BUT YET I ALWAYS SCORED,
I SMILED UPON THE TRAPS THAT CAME
WITH ALL THE RAIN THAT POURED,
AND WHEN I WALKED MY FINAL PATH
AND SOFTLY TOUCHED THE GREEN,
THE FLAG WAS RAISED, MY FINAL STROKE
I MADE MY EAGLE DREAM.

FISHING WITH THE OLD MAN

I REMEMBER THOSE DAYS,
WHEN WE USED TO TALK OF LIFE
AMID THE SPRAYS,

WHEN THE FISH THAT WE CAUGHT
WENT FROM TOO SMALL
TO HOW WE FAUGHT,

WE USED TO LAUGH ABOUT WHO FELL WHERE
OR WHO WAS MORE WET,
WHEN FAMILY TIME MEANT
ALL WE COULD GET,

WHEN THE FIGHTS WE HAD
WHILE FISHING DOWN SOUTH,
WAS THE BIG DEAL ABOUT
WHO TOOK THE HOOK OUT OF THE MOUTH,

ONE TIME, MY DAD CAUGHT A FISH
THAT WAS NO BIGGER THAN MY HOOK,
AND WE LAUGHED SO HARD
THINKING ABOUT WHAT WE WERE GOING TO COOK,

I STILL SMILE EVERY TIME I GO FISHING
I TAKE HIS TACKLE BOX AND HIS FISHING ROD
AND HES ALL THAT'S MISSING,

I GO TO THE SAME SPOT WE USED TO FISH
AND STAND ON THE SAME PIER AS HIM,
REMEMBERING HOW THE BEST PART OF FISHING
IS WHEN WE USED TO GO FOR A SWIM,

BUT I FEEL SO CLOSE TO HIM
ON THE WATER AS MUCH AS I CAN,
TEARS ON MY FACE, JUST THINKING ABOUT
FISHING WITH THE OLD MAN.

GONDOLA BRIDE

ONE THAT I SECURE MY LOVE
AS THE SUN SETS ON A VENETIAN CANAL,
HOLDING YOU IN MY ARMS
WITH THE WIND TEASING YOUR CHARMS,
THE QUIET WATER EASES OUR THOUGHTS
AND BRINGS US TO THAT PLACE AGAIN
OF MOONLIGHT KISSES AND FORGET ME NOTS,
WHILE ALL THE FORCES OF FREEDOM
AGAINST THE HISTORIC WALLS OF STONE,
I HAVE DREAMED THIS ONE MILLION TIMES
FLOWING SWEETLY, COMING HOME
GENTLE WORDS ACROSS THE PIER
PLEASURED SMILES FROM EAR TO EAR,
GENTLE TOSS OF A SINGLE OAR,
WHILE HE SINGS THE OLD ROMANTIC SONGS
I HOLD YOU CLOSER EVEN MORE,
AND WITH THE LOVE OF THIS CITY
I ONCE SAW IN SAINT DENIS,
THE GLORIOUS TEARS HAVE BUILT THIS WONDER
AS WE EMBRACE IN VENICE.

HEART OF A SOLDIER.

WE CHOSE TO GUARD THIS LAND WE LOVE
SO WE CAN ALL BE FREE,
WE PLACE OUR LIVES IN OTHERS HANDS
GOD KEEP US SAFE WE PLEA,
THE BOLD, THE BRAVE, THE FULL OF FEAR
THE BATTLEFIELDS WE ROAM,
BROTHERS, SISTERS, FOR OUR FLAG
OUR FAITH WILL BRING US HOME,
WE WORK AMONG THE FEARS OF WAR
AND WE SHALL NOT NEGLECT,
THE UNIFORM STANDS STRONG FOR TRUTH
THIS COUNTRY WE PROTECT,
THOUGH WE MAY DIE SO FREEDOM LIVES
OUR HEARTS HOLD NOT A GRUDGE,
THE WALL OF MIGHT THAT GUARDS YOUR RIGHT
STANDS FIRM AND WILL NOT BUDGE,
RETURN WE WILL, IF GOD ALLOWS
THOUGH WE MAY NOT BE WHOLE,
BUT SOLDIERS, WE WILL SACRIFICE
TO SAVE ONE FREEDOM SOUL.

I DREAM OF A PEOPLE

*F*OR WE ARE ONE
SKETCHED BY THE ARTIST HAND,
WHAT WILL GIVE COURAGE TO LOST HULLS
WILL ONE DAY SAIL THIS FREEDOM LAND,
THE SEAS TELL OF LONGER DAYS
THE HILLS AND VALLEYS HAVE THEIR WAYS,
AND I DREAM OF A PEOPLE
WHOSE HEARTS PREFER AS ONE,
WHERE OUR THOUGHTS ARE JOINED FOR EACH
AND NO BATTLE TO BE WON,
FOR I SEE A DISTANT SMILE
WHERE PEACE IGNITES ALL SOULS OF FATE,
FOR EACH, WHEN TIME REACHES AT THE STARS
ARE LEFT TO KEEPERS AT THE GATE.

I REMEMBER ME

As your spontaneous choices of travel
Be it for bitter or sweet,
I smile with a drop of curiosity and fondness
For I hold you in my heart
Amid my wonders of life,
I see through your fog and mist
I see through your still and twist,
I have always reached for your web
And seeked your weeve,
For I know not of your air of might,
I know not of your unchartered flight,
And though you worry not,
To mark the verses of your lead,
My mind still follows in your steps
Upon our faith we feed,
I know your thoughts of please,
I know your testing of each breeze,
I feel your passion no one sees,

AND THE YOUNG MAN IN YOU
THAT FIGHTS TO PLOT YOUR COURSE IN TIME,
THROUGH YOUR FATHERS EYES,
TIME CARRIES ON
AND THE SUN WILL RISE,
BUT MY GREATEST TASK IN LIFE
IS TO SEE YOU RISE FROM NOT AT WILL,
REMBER MY SON, I LOVE YOU
FOR I AM YOUR FATHER STILL,
AND I HAVE FAITH IN YOU
FOR EVERYTHING IN YOU I SEE,
I AM PROUD OF YOU
WHILE I REMEMBER ME.

JOURNEY HOME

I AWOKE TO SEE THE FACES
OF THE WINDS THAT CHANGE WITH TIME,
UNTIL I WENT TO REST AT LAST
AND PEACE AGAIN WAS MINE.

KEUKENHOF FLUTE

*T*HERE THEY WERE
ROLLING INTO A COLOURED MAZE OF BLISS
ROWS AND ROWS OF DIFFERENT ROSE,
TULIPS COVER EVERY INCH
AWAKE MY WONDERS WITH A PINCH,
THE LAKES SURROUND THE PLOTS OF FUN
SOME SOFTLY RIPPLE
SOME SLOWLY RUN,
LITTLE BRIDGES, DIFFERENT PATHS
TREES THAT FLOAT WHILE ANGELS VIEW,
FRONT AND CENTER, ALL TAKE STAGE
MARCHING GROUPS AND LINES OF TWO,
AND GRASS THAT CUSHION EVERY RIDE
WHILE LITTLE CREATURES TRY TO HIDE,
THE HOUSE OF ORCHIDS
DEMAND THE CIRCUS SIGHTS,
ARE THEY SCENTED
ARE THEY LIGHTS,
AND BUILT AMONG THE GROUNDS SOFT PETALS

A WINDMILL FROM THE AGES BOOK,
WHERE WORK WAS MAYBE SHELTER TOO
AND FOR THE WINDS
THE WORK WAS FEW,
AMONG THE WATERS EDGE, THE SMILING SUN
THE MORE THE LIGHT, THE MORE THE FUN,
MORE LINES OF SOIL, FROM SEED TO SIGHT,
THE SCENTED AIR THAT BRINGS A SMILE
THE QUESTIONS AS WE WALK AWHILE,
CURIOSITY, FOR THE COLOURED FLIGHTS
SO MANY COLOURS, PEEK AND SEE
SURELY A WONDER AMONG SOULS
MAGNIFICENT STORIES OF EACH AND EVERY REALM,
MAYBE, WHILE LATER DAYS AS I COLLECT MY THOUGHTS
NEAR A BRIDGE OR NEAR A LOFT,
WILL PRIDE THE MAGIC OF A PALETTE PAST
MY HEART WILL SOUND THE BELLS
OF THE KEUKENHOF.

LOVE ALONG THE WATERS OF GROENLO

CAPTURING MOMENTS ON THE BRIDGE
I SEE OUR LOVE REFLECTING ON THE QUIET WATERS
THE EAGLE EYE OF WONDER YEARS,

HOW TWO PEOPLE OF JOINED HEARTS AND TRUE
SILENT TEARS OF ME WITH YOU.

SO SHE WAS MY LOVE BY GROENLO
STROLLING WITH MOVING PEACE,
AND I RECALL,

I TREASURED EVERY MOMENT I HELD YOUR HAND
AS YOU SOFTLY SPOKE WITH YOUR MAGIC WAND,
I KISSED THE YEARS THAT BROUGHT US BY
A KISS THAT WOULD BURN AN ETERNAL FLAME,
AND OURS IS HER
MADE OF LOVE AND JOINED BY WRITTEN WILL BE,
THE PASSION OF OUR LIVES
FOR WE WERE TWO AND NOW WERE THREE,
MY NEARNESS TO YOU WAS A WORLD THAT KEPT ME SAFE
I COULD EXPLAIN TO ME THE FEELING OF FREEDOM TO
KEEP
AND ALTHOUGH IT SEEMS TO BE PURE AND TRUE
I KNOW HOW SWEET WATERS CAN BE DARK AND DEEP,
BUT WE ARE JOINED BY A LOVE THAT WILL LAST ALWAYS
WE ARE SOULMATES FOREVER
AND I WILL AWAY WITH THE WINDS AND YOU IN MY
HEART
FOR I WILL LEAVE YOU NEVER.

MY OWN SKIPPER

AS MY BOAT HAS TOSSED FROM DUSK TO DAWN
WITH MY LINES AGAINST THE BLUE,
I'VE SEEN THE TIDES THAT BROUGHT THE FEAST
AND I'VE SEEN WHEN FISH WERE FEW,
I'VE BEEN THE CAPTAIN AT THE WHEEL
WHEN THE HULL HAS TAKEN TOLL,
AND I AM GRATEFUL FOR HANDS ON DECK
FOR I'VE SEEN THE SEAS AND WHAT THEY ROLL,
AND WHILE THE YEARS HAVE PASSED, THE SALTY SPRAYS
THE WINDS APPEAR MORE COLDER,
BUT I STILL FISH, MY ONLY WISH
THOUGH MY BOAT HAS GOTTEN OLDER,
SO WHEN GALE WINDS UPON MY DECK
ROUGH SEAS AND STORMY DAY,
I SMILE UPON THE SEAS OF CHANCE
IT'S WHERE I LEARNED TO PRAY.

OAK AND HEARTS

*T*HERE WAS ONCE A LITTLE BOY
AND ALL HIS TROUBLES HARD TO FIND,
ALTHOUGH VOICES OF BLACK SHEEP
YET HE SMILED, HIS HEART WAS KIND,

HE KNEW NOT OF PARENTS WRATH
NOR TAKING PLEASURE OUT OF FUN,
AND FAMILY WAS ONLY JUST A WORD
HE WAS ALONE AND HE HAD NONE,

WHEN LEAVING HOME FOR SCHOOL OR PLAY
NO SOFT WORDS, BUT JUST IGNORE,
NO WAVES, GOODBYES OR SEE YOU SOON
OR FIX HIS COLLAR AT THE DOOR,

NOR DID HE DINE WITH KIN AT TIME
OR SLEEP THE HOURS IN HIS ROOM,
AND PLAY WITH TOYS IN CHILDLIKE WAYS
FOR HE BECAME A MAN TOO SOON,

AND TO SOME THE THOUGHT OF HIM TO FORFEIT HOPE
SO PROCLAIMED WITH COMMON VIEW,
BUT THROUGH SKIES THAT DARK EACH NIGHT
THERES ALWAYS STARS TO TAKE US THROUGH.

LIFES A GIFT THAT CARRIES SOON
CAN PASS BEFORE OUR EYES,
IT'S NOT THE FALLS THAT MARK OUR FATE
BUT SURELY HOW WE RISE.

P.O.W. LETTER ON A WALL

WHEN THEY FOUND ME, I SAW YOU STILL
THOUGH THEY TOOK MY UNIFORM AND YOUR RING
I FELT YOUR WILL,
WHEN THEY TORTURED ME, I CALLED YOUR NAME
AND WHEN MY FREEDOM FLOWED FROM MY LIFE
I FELT NO PAIN,
THEIR EFFORTS WERE ALL IN VAIN.
WHEN THE DARK CORNERS CONTAINED MY SOUL
WHILE I WEAKENED
TO KEEP YOU IN MY HEART
WAS MY LIVING GOAL,
THOUGH THE SCENT OF THIS HALF SHELTERED PLACE
STOLE MY DIGNITY AND MY PRIDE
OUR TIMES OF LOVE AND LAUGHTER
REMAINED MY ONLY GRACE,
THOUGH MY FAITH IN HAVING ONE MORE BREATH
WAS FEW
OUR CHILD THAT WE BROUGHT TO THIS PRECIOUS LIFE
WAS MY DEEPEST LOVE, OF ME WITH YOU,
FOR IT WAS GODLY,
THOUGH EVERY WORLDLY POSSESSION HAD BEEN TAKEN
THOUGH THE HUMAN PART OF ME HAD BEEN DEPRIVED,
WHILE I DRIFTED TOWARD OUR FINAL PLACE OF PEACE,
THEY COULD NOT TAKE AWAY OUR LOVING MEMORIES,
THEY ALL SURVIVED,
SO AS I HONOUR OUR JOINED LOVE WITH SACRED VOWS
I WILL COURAGEOUSLY GO, WITH YOU ALWAYS ON MY MIND,
TO A PLACE OF PEACE AND YOUR HEART
WHERE PAIN IS FREE AND LOVE IS KIND.

PICTURES IN THE SAND

PLEASE TELL ME A STORY BEFORE I SLEEP
SO I CAN DREAM A THOUSAND DREAMS,
TELL ME ABOUT THE PRINCESS IN LOVE
WITH HAIR OF GOLD OR SO IT SEEMS,
TELL ME A STORY, IM ALMOST THERE
MY EYES ARE BEGINNING TO CLOSE,
TELL ME ABOUT THE HANDSOME PRINCE
WITH ALL OF HIS TREASURES THAT NOBODY KNOWS,
TELL ME A STORY IM UNDER THE SHEETS
I WANT TO HEAR MORE OF THE STARS,
TELL ME OF ROCKETS AND HOUSES IN SPACE
PLEASE TELL ME OF VENUS AND MARS,
AND TELL ME THE STORY OF FISH THAT COULD TALK
AND LIONS AND TIGERS WITH WINGS,
TELL ME OF BIRDS THAT COULD FLY ME UP HIGH
OVER MOUNTAINS AND VALLEYS AND THINGS,
TELL ME THE STORY OF ALL OF MY LIFE
AND WHAT I WILL BE WHEN IM GROWN,
WILL THERE BE SUNSHINE ON ALL OF MY DAYS
AND WILL I HAVE ICECREAM WITH CONE,
SO TELL ME A STORY BEFORE I AM SLEEPING
OF CANDY STORES ALL IN A ROW,
TELL ME OF RAINBOWS THAT COLOUR MY DAYS
AND TELL ME OF MOUNTAINS WITH SNOW.

RACHELS FLIGHT

*I*N THAT MOMENT YOU KNEW ME
WE JOINED THE BEATING HEARTS OF TRUE,
NO WORDS, JUST SMILES AND THOUGHTS
MY LIFE SURVIVED BY ONLY YOU

DEEP IN LOVE AS WE PASSED FEW YEARS, TOO SOON
BUT ALWAYS A BLINK AWAY,
OFF TO A JOURNEY I WOULD NEVER KNOW
PAINTING LEOPARDS, DAY BY DAY

FOR ROSEDALE WAS A PLACE TO ME
WHERE CHILDHOOD WONDERS CRIED MY TRAILS,
OFF TO SWEET SHEEP AND GODS WATCH
MANY VIEWS AND MANY TALES

THE HAND THAT GUIDES AND KEPT ME SAFE
WAS A WARMTH I CAME TO KNOW,
AND FROM YOUR HEART I ALWAYS FELT
A MOTHERS TOUCH, AS I DID GROW.

RIBBONS BY DAY

WITH A SONG IN MY HEART AND A SMILE ON MY FACE
THE RED ONE WAS CHARMING AND ALWAYS IN PLACE,
THE BLUE WAS AS DIFFERENT AS ALL OF MY TOYS
WHEN I WAS IN PLAYGROUNDS AND PLAYING WITH BOYS,
THE BLACK ONES WERE SHOULD DO'S AND WHAT WE
SHOULD NOT
WHEN MIXED WITH WHITE CIRCLES TO FORM
POLKA-DOTS,
THE PURPLE WAS ENVY WITH STYLE AS IT GOES
ALL BLENDED WITH FASHION AND MATCHING MY
CLOTHES,
THE YELLOW WAS SUNHINE WHEN I WENT TO PLAY
AND MATCHING MY HAIR IN THE HEAT OF THE DAY,
THE WHITE WAS FOR WINGS OF THE ANGELS THAT FLY
AND FLOATING WITH CLOUDS AS THE TIME PASSES BY,
AND THE PINK IS FOR PRECIOUS WHILE HOLDING MY
CURL
IN THE ARMS OF MY DADDY AS HIS LITTLE GIRL.

SAILING HOME

"*T*hough the fair winds goad the seas
And ports are not by choice,
I roll each wave with pride and worth
As I sail towards my mother's voice"

SAME OLD TIMES

*I*M HOLDING ON TO YESTERDAY
WHEN YOUNGER TEENS AND TINY TOTS,
AS GARDENS GROW, THE AGES SHOW
HIBISCUS AND FORGET ME NOTS,
KEEPING SMILES WITH CHRISTMAS TOYS
AMID THE PLAYGROUNDS FUN AND NOISE,
WHEN THE SUMMER CRYSTALS WARMED THE BEACH
IN SILKEN SANDS WE PLAYED,
AND TAKING CARE WAS OUT OF REACH
WITH FRIENDS THAT ALWAYS STAYED,
PROM COLOURED SUITS AND EVENING GOWNS,
AN ENGLISH CLASS WITH VERBS AND NOUNS,
I REMEMBER WHEN MY GRANDMAS BAKES
WOULD FILL THE AIR WITH LOTS OF CAKES,
I STILL KEEP THOSE TIMES OF FUN
AS THROUGH MY LIFE I STRIDE,
I SMILE TO THOUGHTS OF YESTERDAY
IT'S SOMETHING TIME CANT HIDE,
SO WHEN MY NOW FALLS BACK TO THEN
AS MY TODAY IS LOST IN PART,
FORGIVE ME IN MY GOLDEN YEARS
IT'S COMFORT TO MY HEART.

SIFTING

I HAVE OFTEN WONDERED
WHAT TRULY MAKES THE WORTH OF ONE,
FOR IN SHADOWS, IN DARKNESS
THERE ARE THE STRENGTHS OF MANY,
FOR IT IS TRUE,
RELENTLESS IN THE PRIDE AND SELF WORTH THAT
ACHES,
CHARTERED COURSES OF TIME,
THE SORROW EYES ALONG LIFES PATH,
THE HEART THAT PUMPS THE TRUTH TO ME,
BUT I SAW THE BREAKING SKY
WITH PASSAGE LIGHTS WATCHING TIME BYE,
MAY ETERNAL REST SORT THE DAYS COUNT
AND LEAVE ME TO CONTINUE ON THIS JOURNEY,
WITH FAINT CONTENT, AND SUTTLE MOTIONS
SAVOUR THE BEAUTY IN MY THOUGHTS OF MORE AGES
TURNING TEARS AND WINDY PAGES,

TAKE ME TOWARD A PLACE
WHERE I CAN FINALLY CALL HOME,
PEBBLED PATHS, BUT TAKE ME
SCATTERED MINDS THAT GIVE ME HOPE,
FOR I, MISSING LULLABYES AND FEARSOME CRIES
WILL BE ON THAT FIELD OF FAITH,
PONDERING,
REMEMBERING YOU AND WILL YOU REACH FOR ME,
AND THOUGH YOU SEE ME NOT
THOUGH THE SHAME MAY CAST YOUR DOUBT,
I WILL NOT LEAVE YOU
I WILL NOT ABORT MY SORROWS TURNING SWEET,
FOR I KNOW OF THAT LAND I BREATHE
AND WHAT IS FAIR AND WHAT IS TRUE,
THOUGH RAIN AND STORMS MAY FIELD THE FRONT
I WILL NOT LOOSE MY WINGS FROM YOU.

SONGS IN THE MEADOW

WHEN THE COLD CEASES HER TIRED STILL
AND THE FROST IS GONE, NOW CLEAR TO SEE,
FROM WHERE I AM UPON A HILL
THE BUTTERFLIES DANCE IN FLIGHT AND GLEE,

THE ICICLES MELT AND GRASS WILL GROW
WHILE LEAVES IGNITE WITH OPEN FACE,
THE LAND NOW TAKES THE SEEDS I SEW
FRESH SCENTS OF FLOWERS GRANTED GRACE,

I AM YOUR ALWAYS HOST OF DAY
YOU CHARM MY EYES WITH FREEDOM AIR,
WHILE WARMTH DELIGHTS AND CHILDREN PLAY
GREY IS GONE AND SUN SHALL CARE,

AND HEARTS BEAT TO A NATURES DRUM
ALIVE TO BEAUTY, SPRING APPEAR,
IT'S TIME FOR BUD AND BLOOM TO COME
WHILE BIRDS DO SONG IN MEADOW AIR.

A KIND SEASON

WHEN I FOUND THE FREEDOM TO BE ME
THE HAZE LIFTED,
WHEN I FOUND THE VALUE IN DIFFERENCE
THE WORDS THAWED,
WHEN THE WINDS OF TIME SLOWED MY WILL
I TOOK SHELTER IN THE FOG,
WHEN I BEGAN TO UNDERSTAND EQUALITY
I BEGAN TO APPRECIATE THE FOUR SEASONS,
WHEN I BEGAN TO CRY
I WATCHED THE RAINS GIVE LIFE,
WHEN I WAS LOST
THE TREES WERE MY SHELTER,
WHEN I NEEDED MY THOUGHTS
THE STILL WINDS GAVE ME PEACE,
WHEN I LOVED
THE SUN WARMED MY HEART,
WHILE I SLEPT THROUGH DARK TIMES
YOU WERE MY BRIGHTEST DREAM.

THE FREEDOM TO LIVE

I WAS BLESSED UPON THIS PEACEFUL EARTH
WHERE I CAN GAZE AMONG THE FIELDS,
WHERE PEOPLE OF GOODWILL CAN WALK WITH EASE
AMONG THE HEAVENS CROP IT YIELDS,
A PASSERBY, THOUGH BIRDS DO FLY
I SEE A PALE STONE FOG SET IN,
THE WILL HAS LAID THE WREATH OF HOPE
A TIME TO LOVE, A TIME TO WIN,
A SETTING SUN, A FLOATING MOON
DIRECTS THROUGH BREEZE AND WOODS A TUNE,
BUT I WILL BE MY EARTHLY WATCH
AMONG THE LASTING SEEDS IN PLACE,
FOR WE AS ONE, THE AIR WE BREATHE
THE HARSH WINDS OF THE DAYS WE FACE,
FOR WE ARE STILL THE HUMAN RACE.

TILL A PERFECT DAY

REACHING OUT TO HOLD YOUR HAND
AS YOU WHISPER TIMES OF TRUTH,
THE STRONGER HEART PRESERVES ALL PEACE
AS I LEARNED IN MY YOUTH,
THE STORY BOOK THAT HAS NO END
BUT ALWAYS TELLS A TALE,
WILL KEEP OUR MEMORIES LASTING AS
THE WINDS OF FOREVER SET SAIL,
I SEE YOUR EYES, I FEEL YOUR CRIES
KIND RIVERS WILL ALWAYS FLOW,
FOR ALL IS ANSWERED IN DUE TIME
FOR THIS I SURELY KNOW,
AND AS THE SUN GOES DOWN TO REST
THE NIGHT BEGINS TO SAY,
YOUR TENDER LOVE HAS MADE IT ALL
SEEM LIKE A PERFECT DAY.

TILL IM HOME

*T*HOUGH THE DAY WAS LONG AND TOOK ITS TOLL
IT'S NOW GONE AND FORGOT,
MY HEART IS IN ITS RESTING PLACE
MY LOVE, FORGET YOU NOT,
NOW IN YOUR ARMS YOU COMFORT ME
AND PUT OUT ALL THE FIRE,
BUT WHEN IM HOME, THOUGH I MAY ROAM
YOUR ALL THAT I DESIRE,
WAS UP BEFORE THE SUN CAME OUT
AND BACK WHEN IT WAS DARK,
I WATCH YOUR EYES AND SOFTLY SPEAK
AND LOVE IS MY REMARK,
THIS PRECIOUS HOME THAT COMFORTS US
OUR PICTURES ON THE SHELF,
MEANS MORE TO ME THAN LUNCH OR TEA
THE OFFICE AND THE WEALTH,
NOW STAY BESIDE AND BE MY WARMTH
I SIT WITHOUT A PEEP,
SO I CAN SEE YOU IN MY DREAMS
WHILE I GO OFF TO SLEEP.

TILL TOMORROW MY LOVE

BEFORE I CLOSE MY EYES TO SLEEP
I WANT TO SOFTLY SAY,
NO DREAMS CAN MATCH YOUR WARMTH WITH ME
BESIDE ME AS YOU LAY,
ANOTHER DAY HAS GONE AGAIN
AND THOROUGH IT ALL A SMILE,
THE SUN CAME DOWN, THE COOL WIND PASSED
AS I WALKED WITH YOU A MILE,
I THINK OF DAYS GONE BY WE MET
AND ALL THE HOLDING IN YOUR ARMS,
FOR I AM A LUCKY MAN TO SHARE
YOU'RE LOVING HEART AND CHARMS,
YOUR EYES AT MINE, I FEEL YOUR BREATH
MY HAND THAT TWINES YOUR HAIR,
YOU'RE WORDS OF TRUTH THAT CLING TO ME
AS WE GENTLY FLOAT THE AIR,
SO GOODNIGHT MY LOVE, IM HERE WITH YOU
THROUGH FLOATING CLOUDS AND STARLIGHT DOVE,
WE CLOSE OUR EYES AND HOLDING HANDS
AS WE DRIFT OFF FAR TO LANDS OF LOVE.

TRUSTING MISS REID

*I*T TOOK A HEART LIKE YOURS TO HELP
ANOTHER CHILD EACH DAY,
I SAW YOU IN MY DARKEST TIMES
I SAW YOU WHEN I PLAYED,
I FOUND THE ROADS THAT LED ME THROUGH
THE MANY HOURS OF TEARS,
YOU OFTEN HELD MY HAND IN LOVE
AND GOT ME THROUGH THE YEARS,
YOU GAVE ME HOPE SO I COULD REACH
THE DREAMS I KNEW WOULD STAY,
AND AS I FELT THE THORNS OF LIFE
YOU GAVE ME FAITH TO PRAY,
THE YEARS HAVE GONE TO YESTERDAY
BUT MY HEART IS LONG AND I STILL SEE,
MY WINTER HAT AND WINTER COAT
A GIFT FROM YOU TO ME.,
SO HERE I AM, IM ALMOST DONE
AND YOU'RE STILL IN MY HEART,
YOU'RE ALL I HAD AND ALL I TRUSTED
AROUND THE TREE, A BARK.

WADING IN STREAMS

*I*F YOU HAVENT GENTLY STOOD IN STREAMS
WILD, THE RIVERS RUN,
AMONG THE SALMON AND THE TROUT
HOLDING SUN RAYS AND WARM DAYS,
TRICKLING, BUBBLING, SPLASHING,
FLOATING TWIGS AND MINNOWS DASHING,
BALANCING ON SOFT SMOOTH STONES,
MOSSY ONES AGAINST FALLING RIVERBANKS,
ONLY SOUNDS OF RUNNING FREE,
THINKING PAST THE QUIET WORDS,
DIFFERENT FLIES, NO NEED THE WISE
TIMELESS FOR A TUG,
SLIPPERY FLOORS OF UNDER DOORS,
SLIGHTLY COOL IN POETS POOL,
WHERE DID THE TIME GO
IM IN A DAZE OF YESTERDAY,
THE SCENT OF WET RIVER LIFE,
IN THEIR WORLD A CLOSER FEEL OF GUSHING EASE
TO TOUCH IS TO BE,
CLINCHING MEMORIES
STANDING IN A WORLD SO FREE.

WHISTLING POPS

THE OLD MAN STROLLS DOWN MEMORY LANE
HIS EYES ARE FOCUSED HIGH,
HANDS IN HIS POCKET, THE YEARS ARE BLURRED
WITH A WHISTLE AND WINK AND A SIGH,
HIS WIFE HAS PASSED AND HIS DOG HAS TOO
HE REMEMBERS WHEN HE WAS A BOY,
BUT AS FAST AS THE YEARS, SOON CAUGHT WITH THE
TEARS
MANY DAYS WITH HIS WIFE WAS HIS JOY,
IT'S A LONESOME TRAIL AS THE SUN COMES TO SET
THE YEARS HAVE TAKEN ITS TOLL,
FOR BEING A MAN, HAVING ALL THAT HE CAN
AND ALL THAT'S LEFT IS HIS SOUL,
AS HE BOLDLY TAKES THE OLDER YEARS
WITH HIS CHILDREN AT HEART AND THEIR TOTS,
HE BRAVELY WALKS TO HIS FINAL BOW
WITH THE TUNES OF WHISTLING POPS.

ZEBRAS REACHING RAINBOWS

STANDING ON A HILL WITH EYES TOWARD A MAGICAL
SCENE
AND TAKING THE WONDER OF IT ALL,
I COULD REACH OUT AND TOUCH YOUR PAINTED
PALLETS
MAYBE IF I WERE TALL,
MY BLACK AND WHITE HAS STOOD ALONE
WHILE I MARVEL YOUR MULTICOLOURED ARC,
YOUR LIGHT BOUNCES LIKE POPPIES IN FIELDS OF BREEZE
LIKE ALL THE FLOWERS IN A PARK,
YOUR SPECTRUM OF LIGHT IGNITES THE OPEN SKY
AS I GRAZE IN FIELDS OF STILL,
BUT I WOULD NOT CHANGE MY TONES FOR YOU
THIS IS MY WORLD, ITS WILL,
I SAW YOU FORM NIAGARAS STUNNING SPRAY
AND HEARD THE TALES OF GOLD THAT LAY YOUR END,
WHATEVER COLOURS GRACE OUR EYES
REFRACTED LIGHT, ON THAT IT WOULD DEPEND,
OUR COLOURED STRIPES DEFINE OUR VIEW
AS WE WERE CAST SINCE BIRTH,
BLENDING IN THIS WORLD WE SHARE THE WALK OF LIFE
WHILE YOU PAINT THE ART OF EARTH.

SMALL PASSIONS OF POETRY

I TOOK THE WORDS FROM THE VALLEYS AND STREAMS,
I TOOK MY INSPIRATIONS FROM JOURNEYS AND DREAMS.

YOUR FRIENDSHIP WILL FOLLOW ME ONTO THE
BATTLEFIELDS OF LIFE
AND I WILL RELISH VICTORY, IN YOUR HONOUR.

REMEMBER ME WHILE YOU TRAVEL
SPEAK TO ME IN YOUR THOUGHTS
BE THE LOVE IN THE SPARKLE OF THE STARS.

I LEAVE TO MANKIND, MY PLOUGH AND MY CART
AND TO YOU MY LOVE, I BEQUEATH MY HEART.

ROMANCE THE SEAS AND TREASURED PEARL
FOR I HAVE FOUND MY ISLAND GIRL.

YOUR FRIENDSHIP STEERS MY SHIP TO SHORE
WHILE MY LOVE WILL WATCH AT HARBOURS DOOR.

WHEN HUNGER AND THIRST HAD GLAZED MY
CURIOSITY
I KNEW I HAD FOUND HUMILITY.

WHERE THERE IS LIFE, THERE IS LOVE
WHERE THERE IS THOUGHT, THERE IS HOPE
WHEN THERE IS FAITH, THERE EXISTS UNITY.

WITH EVERY WARMTH OF YOUR BREATH YOU SHOW ME
WITH EVERY WORD FROM YOUR HEART, YOU KNOW ME.

I SAID I LOVE YOU, WITH A KISS AND A SMILE
FLOAT WITH ME ALWAYS, FROM NOW TILL AWHILE.

AN ARTIST OF LIFE, YOUR SOFT BRUSHES CREATE NEW
WORLDS
WHERE IMAGINATIONS JOURNEY ON INTO CRYSTAL
COLOURS.

THANK YOU FOR THAT SOFT TOUCH THAT ASSURES ME
THE TIMES THAT YOU TOOK MY JOURNEY
AND MADE IT ALL WORTHWHILE.

WITH EVERY BREATH BE YOUR TRUTH OF TODAY
WITH EVERY WORD, BE YOUR VALUE IN WHAT YOU SAY.

WHEN MY HAND MEETS YOURS AND NO MORE I ROAM
MY FONDNESS FLUTTERS
FOR NOW IM HOME.

SING ME A LULLABYE WHEN I AM TO SLEEP
BUT ALLOW ME MY COURAGE WHEN THE WATER RUNS
DEEP.

AS I WANDERED THROUGH MY THOUGHTS, MEASURING
WEAKER THINGS
I FOUND MY EASE IN WHAT NATURES BEAUTY BRINGS.

THIS MOMENT IS OURS, INTO ONE WORLD WE GO
OUR LOVE ALWAYS JOINED
WHEREVER THE WIND MAY BLOW.

WHILE WE MOVE IN TIME AND EASE, WE PAUSE
REMEMBERING THOSE WHO PROTECT OUR FREEDOM
FOR THE CAUSE.

I AM YOUR QUIET STILL BESIDE YOU
YOU AMAZE ME WITH YOUR HEART
YOU'RE SMILING SHADOW THAT HAS NO END.

LET YOUR SOFT WORDS FOLLOW ME INTO AFTER
REMEMBER OUR TIMES, REMEMBER OUR LAUGHTER.

YOU CAN FILL MY CUP WITH THINGS AND GOLD
BUT AS TWO SECURED BY LOVE
THE SWEETEST STORY EVER TOLD.

YOU ARE MY LAMP ON SHADOWED DAYS
AND THROUGH ALL KINDS OF RAIN,
MY MOTHER, I LOVE YOUR WAYS.

WHEN I KNEW OF MY PATH TO ALWAYS
I SAW THE RIVERS IN YOUR EYES
AND I KNEW OF OUR TRUTH IN US, TO KIND DAYS.

WITH THESE WORDS I SPEAK TO YOUR HEART
TO HUSH AND SOOTHE YOUR JOURNEY
AS YOU READ MY SPOKEN THOUGHTS.

BRIGHT BE THE DAY WHEN PEACE PERFORMS ON
ENDLESS STAGE
WHEN WE EXIST IN UNITY
ANOTHER BOOK, ANOTHER PAGE.

MANY A THOUGHT HAS MOTIONED A SAY
MANY A WORD HAS BRIGHTENED A DAY.

FOR YOU ARE MY FRIEND, MY INSPIRATION, MY REASON
YOU ARE MY TWILIGHT, MY WARMTH, MY SEASON
AND I LOVE YOU.

WHEN SOFT WORDS TUNE THE MUSIC OF TIME
WERE DANCING ON MAGIC WITH POETS AND RHYME.

YOUR SOOTHING VOICE OF ART
DISPLAYS YOUR BOUNDLESS POETIC HEART.

FOR THE SEAS HAVE CAST CURIOSITY
WHILE THE MOUNTAINS HAVE STOOD WISDOM.

BELIEVE IN YOUR ASPIRATIONS
BUILD YOUR WILL IN YOUR WORLD
AND FORWARD WITH THE WINDS OF TIME.

NOW THE DAY DRIFTS TO ITS PROMISED END
BUT I WILL CHERISH YOUR TRUTH AND LOVE YOUR WAYS
MY LOYAL FRIEND.

WITH YOU BY MY SIDE I CAN WALK FOR MILES
WITH YOU IN MY HEART, I CAN RUN A NATION.

FOREVER I AM THANKFUL FOR YOUR CHARMS
BUT THIS MOMENTS IS MY ALWAYS IN YOUR ARMS.

ARISE WITH THE LOVE AND PASSION OF THE GIFT OF LIFE
BE AT PEACE AND LIVE THE TRUTH OF EACH SUNRISE.

THAT SUMMER SKY THAT BREATHES FOUNTAINS OF LIGHT
MAGNIFIES THE PASSAGES
TOWARDS SAILORS AND NATURES DELIGHT.

THE SOFT PETALS DECLARE YOUR OUTWARD SMILE
AND YOUR ROOTS PROCLAIM YOUR INNER BEAUTY.

OH FOR YOUR RHYME WITH REASONS
THE BEAUTY IT TELLS LIKE THE SEASONS.

SOON, THE FLOWERS SCENT WILL MOVE WITH WINDS OF
TIME
BUT LOVE WILL ROAM FREE
WITH IRISH MIST AND WORDS OF MINE.

SPARKLE ME WITH EYES OF VALLEYS GREEN
AND BE MY WONDER
IN EVERY DREAM.

THE SOFTER THE WORDS
THE SWEETER THE TONES
THE STRONGER THE IMPACT.

RIDING ON RAINBOWS, SMILING WITH SUNSHINE
AND CATCHING YOUR DREAMS,
ANOTHER DAY TO BE GRATEFUL.

POETRY REMINDS US OF THE KINDNESS OF OUR SOUL
AND THE TRUTH OF OUR MEMORIES.

SPEAK SOFTLY WHILE I PAINT YOUR ART
WRITE FREELY, WHILE I FEEL YOUR HEART.

WITH THESE WORDS I HAVE REVEALED
BE OUR LOVE AND BE OUR SHIELD.

POETRY IS A WORTHWHILE JOURNEY OF EXPRESSIONS
CREATING VISIONS OF PEACE
FOR ALL PEOPLE.

POETRY IS THE RHYTHM AND SONGS OF EXPRESSIONS
IN YOUR HEART AND MIND.

THANK YOU TO MY READERS

*T*his is my third book that I am honoured to present to my readers.

It has been truly overwhelming watching the sales of my first two books and I am very grateful for the interest in them both. My passion is to write. To let feelings, situations and emotions come alive in words, in rhyme, in the spirit of love and humanity.

In this my third book, I again try to present the readers with my grateful expressions of life and I look forward to your reviews, whatever they may be. Please take the time to fill in the contact form on my website with your comments.

I look forward to our years of friendship.

Author Kenny Lord

apoet.ca

Never lose the faith in your heart,
the sweet of your soul and the right to smile.

Kenny Lord